nightsong

nightsong

Sundress Publications • Knoxville, TN

Editor: Tierney Bailey
Editorial Assistant: Anna Black
Special Thanks: Aumaine Gruich, Sabrina Sarro, Ada Wofford
Colophon: Text set in Calisto MT, a serif from Monotype Imaging.
Cover Design: Kristen Ton
Cover Art: "Hide Away" by Raven Juarez, ravenjuarez.com
Book Design: Tierney Bailey

nightsong
Ever Jones

Ever Jones

acknowledgements

The author gratefully acknowledges the editors of the following publications where these poems first appeared, sometimes in different forms:

Poetry Northwest	"when i was a girl..."
Glass Poetry Journal	"how death holds form..."
A Portrait in Blues (anthology)	"interrogation of..." & "silver-specked pumpkins..."
Terrain.org	"the sun made itself to burn..." "raven's wings press..." "Coyote howl softens..." "in this new night pronouns..."
Yes, Poetry	"nighttime in the greenhouse..."

contents

Dedicated to queer & trans folx—those thriving, surviving & those gone

Written between the Pulse nightclub mass shooting
and Barack Obama's final day as president
June 12, 2016 – January 20, 2017

gnats made of light cast spells
in sycamore's stadium of needles

the ones who know they have a body
know that spring is sudden & burns
the edges

that leaning into the waves of bark

gives up the body

pulseshadows
a standing ghost

the sun made itself to burn

    a long death, a cloud around the equator

        my waist

      a stone
     the poem stalls

   tender skin

horizons want resources for the human wish

   see the sun lower golden pennies

    see me walk there offering peonies
        an invocation

    through a sheath of violence orbiting my body, my body

  the sex of sunlight
  the gender of bone

i see dead
trans bodies
as crushed stars on snowshadows

  (there's a feeling here
  don't name it)

i see the living
trans bodies
as crushed stars putting away the hammer

sun came and named the planet
a wolf's stare

my body registered animal

Swainson's Thrush returned drawing circles
with its trill, a sticky tongue
in the forest i die in

she is my former pronoun, a circular elegy

found my spirit
curled in my neck

stretched it with promises of spring grass
& believing that this life has some reason
for mornings & the nouns they find

i promised
that i wouldn't build another box
to lie in

that my gendered body would be more
than a 6-foot silence

interrogation of swallows between the sky & i
—a transnoun: a bird, a taking

an acceleration of emptiness
between

    my breasts, a lament

        i see wildness as *a quality*
           close to death

        (the barnacle shell carved of its last dead pieces
                            inside me
        teaches the seaweed how to live)

    when they are no longer there (my breasts)

      i will sing love of their elegy

          memorizing the chest length scar as
              a necessary violence

      a hole so hollow a howl crawls in

the earth on its spindle

the nearwind of cosmos gathers the orbit of my neck

to see suddenly pieces of my body in atomic arrangement

winter skin sloughed in the sun

the whirl of my dissolution is a love i cannot explain

i'd bring you in if i could
into this love for death
in which nothing ever happened

the mother speaks to her child like a child

though he is a golden sea star
one arm on beauty, the other violence

(the ocean's only light is this one)

the other arms twisting around himself, winding thread

into a mass of love too bright to be seen

bodiesdown/spiritsup
let our ancestors let

    let our letting draw us

into the single circle
Celan saw when poems were reduced to narrow tears

        where meaning
            slipped in

      they died alive:

      pulsing bodies
      nearer to life than any bullet/poem

so when fallen

    galaxy's spaces

    made room for them

while our earthly life began to forget
the reason for the wound

at the vigil we brought the stars down
from the sky

our pronouns rinsed wordshadows

into the graveyard of ancestors kill-
ed to prove the sky's whiteness

in this moment of silence, a word is deathless
so your body swallows time, mixing

and unmixing, being transbeing, a shooting
                              *
                         *   *
                            *   *

how death holds form, a beholding

    or more accurately: how an elegy holds the body with words

        i cannot tell you how i already know

        the butterfly, or how i recognize its body

          on the roadside, wind

            bristling the stillness
            as if spirit remains/be/holds

        or the numbers giving in to gusts

        or the ampersand between its wings

      i cannot tell you anything of the world of dying

    except that blackberry is pungent as it blisters

      & that the sliding dust of umber from its wings?

        i can tell you it planted a comet in my eyes

dusk is an oracle thrush foretelling

        the body bathed in early midnight

              this is less about being forgotten

    which is to say losing you is another fire

if every death is ours to carry, then make us

        wings from a song
        until the moon is a silver carcass

i only wanted to hold a moment

        in my fangs until it hissed,

            watch it ache to be wild

when i was a girl

night told me to bite or burn

      my ass was a cat call, my face a baby, my hips

a handle – my body's object turned skin to ash

           when i was a girl i was

                a pearl gathering itself from dust
                a wordsong waiting in a shell

        how can i tell you that your eyes are commas

      in my obituary where every cathedral is a stranger

that every time you argue my grammar

      after tracing my breasts from moon into tit

      or citing the manual of singulars & plurals

my spirit folds its syntax into a choke

      dear silence

           wingmuscle pulls down the air's stars
           opening each throat in the meadow

      dear silence

           windsong releases the throats of the dying
           until each sound is a resting place for gods

dear silence

    we burn too brightly for the boundaries of nouns
most days we'd give it all up to be a fire

under the plum tree a red lineage

    spreads our history with pulp & skin

      —tongue-red, marrow-red, complicated-red the blood

        my ancestors took from yours–truth-
                        red

          your blood

          my silence

some days each question i ask scrapes

    the pulp along the knife's tip
    for another hundred years

    forges nothing and forgets everything:
        tree, root, rain, sun, soil, flower, bud, flesh, skin
        a systemic supremacy or an old plum tree

  see?

      under the plum tree a red lineage

      spreads our history

  my ancestors shook the tree
          violently

  then gave me their hands

in the myth
a dragon collects sorrows at the edge of the world

    near the moon pulling heart beats into hawks

        (sorrows are as old as birth, the first cry
        into the empty universe that never
        reserved space for us)

a dragon attached to me once, feeding

on a season of sorrows when i didn't want to live
here

when the weight of human violence
revealed spectrums of brutality & extinction
& the transbeing inside my body burned too hot to hide

    so i spoke to it, the dragon

        by tracing its image on paper

        & saw my mother

            burned by the world for her madness

        & saw my ancestors

hanging & hanged

of sorrow, Rilke wrote: *if drinking is bitter, become wine*

    so i took in the dragon & swallowed our sorrows

        a rose-colored inheritance at the edge of the world

raven's wings press the living
into evening's long shadows

      that unhinge from the meadow as coffin lids
      might open for the one with sorrow

          have you wondered how the raven's human voice

            is an usher

                in a world of sun?

          the shadows walk—or is it float?—to the creek

        where the salmon were, and kneel into its scrapbook

          of lives neatly fixed at the corners

         the light of billion-year-old plankton unfolds
         its singular cell into a mirror of spines

have you wondered why we follow the raven
to the other side of night

          while it has little care for our created

            world, spare a few scraps

         on the surface of our knowing?

—owl's silent breach of air produced an anonymity

     if pronouns must be in agreement with their subjects
     then i was made weather, a stretching infinitve

        any/body was the forecasted singularity
        every/body and no/body the storm
        until the lonely silence before
        opened the sky and some/body was rain

but what if the owl opened my body to a plural indefinite pronoun

     my body both the storm and silence
     my body a few bodies: a flower, a meadow and the rain
     my body a many: the molten core, the chorus of stones,
     composting the bodies of roots & hooves & paws
     & rain & storm water & the storm & weather—

        (this brief illusion between the stars that are my body, too)

yet if my indefiniteness were both singular & plural, then i'd pull
the world into my body

     my body the all that ever was

     my body the any becoming the sun

     the more a pronoun expanding edges

     the most a majority pronoun agreeing on everything

     i would be one, composing & dissolving endlessly

Coyote howl softens the air into aria

      & an apple thumps the ground with nightsong

        we don't know why the leaf suddenly shivers

        or which paw snapped the blackened stick

    but we stay in their echoes until the wound

passes like a sieve of humid air

      i am loved here

        in the moon's half-phase

          you shining the stars for me

        making the galaxy just another walk to the sink

      in this new light an owl settles on the ledge beyond sight

        giving me a silence far more salient than any word

cold front moves in to my throat

  spreading thin blue light across its palette

    of roots & soil that curl with moonlight

  i taste the slate of mineral horizons

    & the salty isolation of the red cedar

  holding the forest together with its will for depth

they say blue light burns the flesh for a clean wound

  so i drink the carbon shared by each sapling

& hear the near sounds of a family washing dishes

  they say the thyroid is a butterfly

    whose wings gather the wind into a song

  so i rest here cauterized in the long tone of trees

silver-specked pumpkins reach through vine
& shadow the night in arms

a lover hums a hymn of desire
near the edge of waking

last night a trans woman was murdered, her
undrawn constellation

lit a flame in a room that had forgotten itself

we return and return to this field to find a desire
unblemished by the images that contain it

did you know that constellations are drawn
from darkness?

that the milky way casts shadows on us
in the shape of birds?

i collapse my body inside feather & down
redrawing the galaxy of celestial bodies

the blood of an alder is viscous sap

whose smokescreen is

a stunned boy in Aleppo

i remember in Donkey Kong

how we'd use a joystick

to jump barrels

hurled at us

some barrels became fireballs

different from blood

but still the redflames

in the game we'd receive

an extra life

for rescuing the damsel

or would simply begin again

at Level 1

practicing our training in white american heroism

the boy was watching a barrel

hurled at him from thesky

filledwithshrapnelandchemicals

he was on Level 2

which is to say he is stunned to be alive

the blood of the barrel

a hot thorn in his skin

sticky as oil my fingertips

pressing *reset reset reset*

dark water slid forward in ribbons

slipping through my body submerged

my fingers stroked sunset on its surface

making ink drop impressions in the watercolor-rose

that remembered me without borders

two kinds of clouds caught the horizon

the furthest a dragon twisted deep in ember

the other the blue-gray drift of an empty torso

when O'Keefe's vision faded she began to see

from the sky's perspective, a blended reality

see there the water pulling sunset from a womb

the single feather of the flame-colored tanager

sweeping edges into the deep currents below

ékleipsis means to abandon as in giving up
the ghost you love for your life

        six thousand people die in the hour
        of the antumbra's foggy halo

eight species go extinct during the temporary darkness
of finding yourself

        in this brief moment of unknowing
        touch your cheek like a stranger

        if every breath is a spark, breathe fire

climb inside the ring before it abandons
feel the sun's edges burn your holy skin

        until you fall apart
        & come back again

in this new night pronouns unbecome the body

letters shake loose their coats into ravens
slanting syntax under feathers

pull each system from your/self

noxious weeds   strangling   the cedar

punctuation's   teeth
sunk
in the ground

& unwind the human gaze leveraging gravity
into supremacy

when Goddess Diamond picks up the letters
in the new sunrise

see a prism of curves

each serif a hooking talon
every comma a new way to feel rain

(the shape of a bird
pinioned above a cauldron of secrets

a dress made from dismantled sentences

      the throat of raven
      is sunrise
      too bright for any
            noun

         wilderness
         synthesizing into sea

      black ants carving
      an overripe peach

      so tender
      the thumb's shape)

i remember sudden breasts on my boychest
and the white training bra without instructions

on what i was training for. what i want to write
about is how we love each other, but instead

soft cup, underwire, plunge, strapless, sport,
push up. the instructions just say to fasten

the clips. how we love each other is not
enough, over the shoulder boulder holder,

boomerang, sling-shot, tit sling, cleavage
commando. the man said *nice tits*, but i

didn't have any yet. my instructions
to respond had not been given to me.

it's just that if anyone had loved me enough
to ask i'd have said that breasts will slowly kill me.

begin by securing the clasp around your ribcage,
rotate the clasps to the back then pull your

arms through the straps and tighten. hooters, racks,
puppies, the twins. the boy grabbed my chest,

reported to his friends that i may not be a girl at all.
it was an assault but what i'd been training for all along.

i love you, a wound in body's spaces
the snake's coil filled with stars

it begins here: in the where of *I am*

which is dusk pouring us golden

—leaves, wings, teeth a primordial gesture

did you see?
my pencil made a mark to save us

but found the sun spinning a comet
like a tetherball around us

i don't think the world waits for answers

someone's late summer wish drifts at my feet

       dandelion seed snuffed into a room
       forgotten by its pictures

            last night when the boygirl made out
            with the starcrush

                  i saw the moon dismember the ocean

                  into billions of underwater bodies

no one else saw the sky fall between their lips

            or walked home kicking stars
            slowly down the road

then rain turned the ground

    we fell into it

        the election
        of false words

        paper leaves
        at children's feet

        we forgot the iron core
        how it melts into a massive heart

    and Venus' cloudcloak
    a saccharine narrative

love i'ed and you'ed
into a bloody pulp

        you singe at the request
        pounding her chest
        hoping the myth releases

another body found
      world-silent

in the rosemary halls
      of bomb-quiet

blood navigates my body's earth
      a dragon-tooth of sorrows

i fall in love
      through the story-clouds

fusing my animal
      into ground-ocean

settling into a sea of exhalations
      stars time-counting

you can hear it here
      your ear ticking buriedthings
              buriedthings
              buriedthings
              buriedthings
              buriedthings
              buriedthings
              buriedthings

gray current surges the sea forward
    cresting echoes of war's forgotten violence

        (consider the wolf's choices in the human movie:

            to starve on the edges of its being
            or gnaw its own paw to taste its myth)

   where fog meets the sea
   the human wish discovers

       a love greater than but not equal to

       the empty spaces where the body's waters ebb

         (that edge of heartbeat a fang in the neck

          but rain slants the message)

it pelts   :   an animal word
   the stripped body removed from bone

        canines slashing in a jar

        a requiem to drink

every night the world lives through another shadow

　　this is the only hope i carry in this long hall-
　　way of torch light

　　　　my mother is at home tending to a split

　　　　　　mind　　which is to say her body
　　　　　　is a graveyard of roses

　　　　in yesterday's war all the dead bodies rose
　　　　from the sea's tomb

　　lighting the sun's first light with sequins of fire

we looked to it & squinted shame until it squeezed
　　　　　　　　　　　　　　　　　roses

　　　　and we fell under a tree feeling the soft pelt

　　　　　　of animals rise in silence around us

　　my mother didn't learn love until she lost it

　　　　a rabbit she loved, her father, a home
　　　　(she forgot to return from the between spaces)

　　　　　　　strike the match on stone, again

　　　　so history wakes to another reason for living

stars spread their wings releasing snow flakes
        piling crystals on our shoulders

                i brush off an eagle
                & see it land in a pile of silent clocks

        in this countdown to war open your mouth

                to the silent O of time

                        the circle that means nothing when it starts

                except that a god can slip through stillness
                humming aria in the empty field

        the neighbor's inflated snowman

                leans toward what i cannot hear

                        his yard a field of fallen bodies

                i lay my body into generator-echo

                        parallel to santa's sagging face

                to believe in a miracle

        or that the ways of blood may turn the snow to roses

wordsnow in pawprint

the world animal-released

hyphen recreates the body:
androgynous starlight
a fang hooked in a throat

or an angel proving itself
with snowy impressions

the white woman says evil is around any corner
but i only see mirrors hidden in drawers

i've been alone with myself

& can only say i am sorry to have arrived
empty handed

my mouth stuffed with feathers

cleaver is neck-warm

    i pound the avocado pit
    into a green pearl

        my bodyshifts mammal

        i scrape slop to the circling crowd

and remember a blackbird launching its broach into
                the future

    while suddenly sifting my life for a lasting thing

        its beak scissor-stitches a curious stammer
            doing & undoing tired verbs

on the occasion of the last day of my life

    i want the matter of matter to imagine itself lost

        an orchestra of fragments
        cleaved as empty vernacular

a clawed punctua-
tion dredges exclamation
i am here, i'm here!

                    locating myself
                    in pressed language a portrait
                    with blood on the lips

        a wound looking back
        shadow becoming its place
        or a ---------- coffin

                    a wing is fiber
                    or a painting of light, we
                    work our nightsilent lives

to find galaxy
in our eyes, listen to what
you see to see it

a pepper's dim lamp

retreats back to womb

a seed of mirrors

clinging to the central vein

remembering wars, winters and the crystal paws
of wolves moaning their low warning

here, too, i feel a hibernaculum of warmth

the sun collecting in the pockets of these seasonal losses

in this brief time of northern lights

i straighten my spine & hear the election of sparrows
seek congress for survival

& am reminded of our collective illusions

in this season of our species' wintering

nighttime in the greenhouse is a riot

> of flowers
> painting
> love
> letters
> for sky & earth

here, i am a roadside spectator in another's cathedral

> when the knife—or were they *shears*?—sever

> the body

> for another grocery story bouquet

> shall we see this as grave?

noun: an excavation in the earth, a mound, a digger, a secret
adj: grave questions, grave errors, grave news
verb: to dig, to excavate, to bury, to hide, to swallow up

> shall we set a hyphen in our rotational value of being?

> when she said *i will fight tooth and nail*
> did she remember the blood

in our teeth

> the silent chambers of hearts
> and vulnerable jugulars seized

> from every paycheck

or is this her seize

in a world so spun every heart is an enemy

at the flower shop a white father & son select an exceptional
bouquet for mom. they are dressed in full camouflage: desert-meets-
forest-meets-jungle-meets-america-meets-war. the pattern is tooth
and nail, pockets roomy enough for every extinction, each genocide-
attempt. see the grave-trenches honored with wildflowers. if i could
i'd drop this poem into the boy's pocket, but i fear he'd kill me
for my gender resistant body, for the gentle touch of the unknown
that he will never be allowed

                  to be

       my pen tip is a claw, a nail, and i admit
       that i jab myself every day for the admittance
       of my body. the violence of non-gender
       and the safety of white skin: a heart chamber
       seals & releases, seals & releases

did you know that a tusk is a tooth?

  an incisor for shadowing the landgrassestrees

       i think that teeth have memory in the electric circuit
       of their nerves, that nails are graves for the dead
       continuously reimagining the matrix of being alive

            i am trying to write about shootings

                  you see

       but my animal body
       but my animal body

    a tusk lacks enamel, pearly vs. ivory—but has growth rings

around the blood
around the original memory

i think that's what i mean to say about tenderness
i think that's what i mean to say about power

somewhere on the farthest shore my body

    slips past the slow pastel of morning

the sea surging somewhere the sea urging

    a protest torch in moon's knuckle

somewhere my body somewhere body

    where morning silhouettes mountain

and i find my body under the saucer of ice

    that declared itself boundary overnight

between my body the erasing sky my body

    is urging to be bloody/body/abode

a line of prairie fire swallows sideways
breath anticipates the spreading crisis

the orange light is a horizontal wand

spelling a harvest of bodies

a gust tore Monday – Friday

a place between chirp and howl
at the top halves of trees

where a tangle of branches fold your map

(the view is an intimate
wandering of curves)

the right metaphor for madness might be
fire
inside the hollowed tree

flames lunging then stealing away

similar to how we remember war
in these late decades of fiery horizons

my mother hung a CLOSED sign on her
windows long ago

her charred body hollowed by a mind
that couldn't trust the direction of rivers

or the boundaries of fire we control

in chutes & ladders
life is played in 100 squares

rolling the dice
to the bottom of a ladder

plant a seed and receive

the
reward
37
squares
and
a field
of ripe fruit

i wait there

spilling sun-warmed juice down my chin
pulp gathering along my neck

waiting to share the sweet fruit

but everyone passes by

i roll the dice again

sink
down
a
chute
my sluggish
body
sliding
into
a waste land
of sand

and again no one comes

life in the white imagination is a grid refusing the past
or slick feathers wrapped around a heaving breast

      did you see the bluebird's youngest forced
      from its nest? —lost its wing and cried for hours

the made-world is smaller under a grid

      100 squares and an eye is a galaxy

            fixed odds
            9 ladders
            10 snakes—Mallarme's dice roll

                  clacking against the worthless board

    the wing was gray

wind throws a shadow from my body
tosses a spark, salt—the past saying says

    here here, the sun is your rotational value

        hold the moment solar its song is mybody its
        notes become me

      the thee

downy woodpecker composes language into eucalyptus tree
a rosetta stone of evolution, a typewriter pecking bullet letter

      (my fingers here, too, this keyboard, i am
      authoring a question?)

      —i i

want this and this and this and one of those—

      an *i* is not a slice of love but an illusion
      dot your i's says the assimilated wood   pecker

        a labyrinth up and down the trunk and listen
        for history to organize its soldier—

the wind dies but isn't dying, my shadow loves me but
left me for wind

    the wind lights me up an aria in broad dashes

      -- -- -- -- -- --

i slip from your mirror

        carrying my secret there is nothing
only sensation, only the accident of my heart

        touch my neck as it slides down another
question, touch

        my shoulder holding the past in place, as
if the past could ever be touched/again

        touch clavicle & rib cage, touch all the
nothing, feel all that ever was—the wind again

        shapes the mountain, presses the
undulation into me/you,

        the pronoun explodes and your anvils
knock for a song:

        hear it there, an entire mountain over you,
taunting with horizon

        (as if the moon ever waited for the dark)

this is the note to wait for, the agreed upon C, Coltraine's Circle:

    5 parts, 7 notes, a wind painting, a mystic

    does it help me/you sleep. please pour me/us another
cup of coffee with sugar, rich and smooth elucidation,
a chattel stream, a labor force of extinction,
        (exits exits exits)

    here is the silent heart, the rules of acrimony,
the nature poem.

your/self, there's a question here
sharpen it

there's a question at the center of every/thing

thing; thing; go hunting

it is December & rain is a typewriter composing
our losses back to life

& at the poet's café old white men quote the old men
who themselves quoted old white men who
named the original word the quote of white men

& the last autumn leaf lets loose
& the rain writes history for a feast

on the wall in America the portrait of a ruin
in the ruined country a portrait of god

only the dead have seen the end of war

said the founder of white thinking
lost in the hallways of his missing body

all i know tonight is this: to stay alive
is to clutch the poem's flare, pull

the pin, toss it in the bunker
maybe this time it doesn't bury

on the last hour of the last day
when rivers stop & wine runs dry

lay your shadows on the sundials
& on the fields let the winds loose

let the sky open the corn stalk
as the last seed presses below the plow

in summer's late hour, in the sky's release
of firmament he who remembers home

will return the hoe to its resting hook
& see the last seed, a star coming forth

blue heron reveals the night's silence
           a gnarled declaration above the pier
reaching its plank above the cold waters
           mixing our poisons & the poisoned
into a disease of roses in graveyards
           in my headphones my nation's leader
weaves justice and genocide into a silky braid
           one strand, then another & another
uniting citizens into willing hunters
           the heron takes on midnight's blues
under a quarter moon guarding the gate
           between life & the death we carry
its beak a silver stamen under the hunched spine
           where every fish is a soldier
ebbing back & forth in the tangled web we
           believe—after the applause i swear
the moon released a pack of ghostly wolves
           upon the waters to illuminate the last
wild spaces within us—the heron stood guard
           witnessing the circling of our dirty water

from below the ice shelf's crack

ten thousand ghosts
flood the oceans

iceshadows rinsed in methane
will haunt the water's circling geysers

        (the moon left its roses for another grave
        a partial eclipse, a tiny red fire

        i couldn't help but applaud its aptitude for desire)

earlier i tried to find the poem about happiness
but found endless war in the archive's lungs

each click was a choke
in the forest of coughing trees

                i wanted to locate my body
                before it drowned

                but instead found a star in the
                turtle's underwater eye

        reaching into it the planet's map
        absolved me with another legend

            i came up for another breath
            then plunged again for another life

she said when we die, a portal opens
        near the death, so dying is like
        three
            falling
                dominoes

                my brother is afraid of the black & white game
                    how the matching dots develop
                    a labyrinth on the tabletop

we visited mom at the asylum once
        & only remember green walls
        cigarettes & dominoes

                a game played in a silence
                    that never released
                    its sutures over our childhood

sometimes i imagine him standing in Mary Frank's painting
        the one where three black arches
        open like portals

                a shadowy figure beckons with his arm
                    will you come? will you?
                    we see only these three directions:

a birch reaching through a green pastoral,
        a distant empty tunnel
            or the center arch

                where the shadow figure rises from a rowboat
                    man & boat are rendered
                    a single entity

similar to how the fog, sky & shore blend
        into indiscernible realities
        will you come with me?

the question hangs in the air
　　　he wades into the water
　　　asking *have I lived*

the fog under city lights rises with
ghosts from my ancestor's tombs

in every vapor an eye
every glint of light a grave

still i see only separation as origin
the center of earth my only core

when my family left their homes
for empty promises i became reason

for murder, a body turned white
in its lonely game of pretend culture

fog is a layering and I adhere to its depth
reaching my arm in to pull something

of this spirit, an invisible mist
I slide down my neck's question mark

sometimes the dead are what we bathe in
when the moon refuses us, a stay

from evaporation. poem, be a potion,
a salve of starlight, an original word

I'll spread the fog for us until we shimmer
with our animal eyes meeting

somewhere behind us is every nature endlessly cradling

the thorns of our bodies—a green wave

in the gray ocean or the particular mist

binding cells into a holy ground of flowers.

sometimes we speak to ourselves in flowers

erupting morning wisdoms whispering

there, there now, these wounds.

of wounds I know little more than the gaping heart

of my throat, the persistent swallowing of my tongue

and the milk of pain from my country.

but of fog I know the dissolution of edges

& how that Appalachian mountain broke

into a palette of stars each morning. I know

all of this that can poem the present

into pollen, a salve for the liberation

I see ahead of me in the shape of stars & throats.

notes

[interrogation of swallows between the sky & i]: "a quality close to death" is quoted from Susan Griffin

[under the plum tree a red lineage]: "under the plum tree..." is after Natasha Marin

[in this new night pronouns unbecome the body]: Goddess Diamond, a trans woman of color, was murdered on June 5, 2016

[it is December & rain is a typewriting composing]: "only the dead have seen the end of war" is attributed to Plato

thank yous

Thank you to the Coast Salish Tribes of Vashon Island, where most of *nightsong* was written. Thank you also to Plum Forest Farm for caring for a portion of this land after it was stolen through colonization. So much of what you grow is in this book.

Thank you to the Spring Creek Residency & Playa for artistic time and support. Also, thank you to the University of Washington Tacoma, colleagues & students, for continued support.

Thank you to Erin Elizabeth Smith of Sundress Publications for loving poetry and being enthusiastic about this book. And thank you to Tierney Bailey for thoughtful and skilled design that brings *nightsong* together.

For Sarah A. Chavez, friend and critic, thank you for reading & helping *nightsong* find its final form.

For Erin, Rod, Harlan, Rae, Frances, Bunny, Danica, Nancy, Talia, Jane, Lena, Anastacia, Naa, Natasha, JB & Alison for friendship & inspiration during the making of *nightsong*.

For Corinne, a galaxy-sized thank you for your brilliance & clarity & support & love. You always find me when I get a lost. You teach me love.

about the author

Ever Jones (they/them) is a queer/trans writer, artist & instructor based in Seattle. They are the author of three poetry collections, *nightsong*, *Wilderness Lessons*, & *Primitive Elegy*, & won the grand prize for the Eco-Arts Awards. Ever is a Professor of Creative Writing at the University of Washington in Tacoma & teaches at Richard Hugo House. Their most recent publications include *POETRY Magazine*, *Tupelo Quarterly*, *About Place Journal*, & others. Please visit everjones.com to view some art.

other sundress titles

Maps of Injury
Chera Hammons
$16

Lessons in Breathing Underwater
H.K. Hummel
$16

Dead Man's Float
Ruth Foley
$16

Blood Stripes
Aaron Graham
$16

Arabilis
Leah Silvieus
$16

Match Cut
Letitia Trent
$16

Passing Through Humansville
Karen Craigo
$16

Phantom Tongue
Steven Sanchez
$15

Citizens of the Mausoleum
Rodney Gomez
$15

JAW
Albert Abonado
$16

Bury Me in Thunder
moira j.
$16

Gender Flytrap
Zoë Estelle Hitzel
$16

Boom Box
Amorak Huey
$16

Afakasi | Half-Caste
Hali F. Sofala-Jones
$16

Marvels
MR Sheffield
$20

Divining Bones
Charlie Bondus
$16

The Minor Territories
Danielle Sellers
$15

Actual Miles
Jim Warner
$15